Made in the USA
Las Vegas, NV
27 March 2021

20181607R00069